Boat Girl

BERNARD ASHLEY

Illustrated by
Elsie Lennox

HARCOURT BRACE & COMPANY
Orlando Atlanta Austin Boston San Francisco Chicago Dallas New York
Toronto London

For Thinh and Ly Ung

This edition is published by special
arrangement with Walker Books Limited.

Grateful acknowledgment is made to Walker
Books Limited for permission to reprint *Boat
Girl* by Bernard Ashley, illustrated by Elsie
Lennox, cover illustration by Iain McCaig.
Text © 1990 by Bernard Ashley; illustrations
© 1990 by Elsie Lennox; cover illustration
© 1990 by Iain McCaig.

Printed in the United States of America

ISBN 0-15-302221-3

    4 5 6 7 8 9 10   011   97 96 95 94

Contents

1

The letter sent home had warned them no-one went on the School Journey if a parent didn't come to the briefing. So there they were in the school hall, grown-up bottoms overlapping the rims of children's chairs, with just the one sitter who fitted her seat, and that was Kim Lung. She had to be there because her father's English wasn't up to such a meeting where all the details would be given out. He had to have a translator, even after all these years. Now he sat there holding Kim's hand and staring straight ahead, a short man with young hair, ready to dip his head to hers when the time came. Kim eased her hand away, pulled up her already pulled-up socks. She had come into the row of seats first, was on the wrong side of him; and she didn't like holding the hand with the scar on it. Her father let it drop, fingered the scar as he often did, like someone blind reading a story in it, while Kim looked up at all

the adults' faces, feeling very out of place, very small.

The teachers came in and sat behind the trestle table at the front. Mr Holt, the headteacher, nodded and smiled, especially at Kim. It was the look he gave the helpers and the parents, not the stare he usually gave the children.

Kim took in a long breath of hall air and sat up. No, feeling *small* wasn't it. She didn't feel small, she felt short, just miniature: because what she knew about some things was as much as anybody sitting there tonight.

"Letters," Mr Holt said. It was near the end now and even Kim on her chair was uncomfortable. All the School Journey details had been given out and whispered in Vietnamese into her father's ear. It had to be done like this. She could speak the rare language well and understand it. Although she couldn't read it, it was all they spoke at home. She had to translate everything from school because her father couldn't read more than his name in English. There was never much put on paper at Kim's place.

"Letters."

The important stuff was over. Kim made that little 'don't worry' sign translators do when they aren't going to bother. She could give the whispering a rest for a few minutes.

"Write often," Mr Holt said. "Children get very homesick if they don't get letters. Write any nonsense you want – but keep it cheerful." Mr Holt made his old joke. "Don't send sad stuff about going into their rooms and seeing the empty pillow. And if the cat dies tell them about the budgie instead!"

"What was that?" Kim's father demanded.

"Nothing much – about children feeling bad."

Mr Lung looked at her. "It isn't you feeling bad, it's me. No help for a week!"

And the meeting ended, with Kim only too glad that she didn't have to queue at the table to tell them about any medicines, or about wetting the bed. That was something! But not enough. Why couldn't her dad be the same as the rest?

2

She enjoyed the first night: six of them in a little room in bunks, miles away in Wales with a window where you could see the river winding out of sight. A lot better than the brick wall at the back of the Granada which her bedroom faced at home. And a load of laughs they had! Tracy Sargent in a zip-up sleeping suit which looked like an outsize babygro. And Wendy Kent not having enough hands to keep herself private when she got undressed. It was better than sleeping alone above the take-away. In loud whispers they went on about Lee with the ear-ring and a missing front tooth, the boy they all went silly about. Till Mrs Winterburn came in for the third time – really ratty at the last in her dressing gown and hairnet – and suddenly the air became heavy, and loud breathing took over from talk. Kim was probably the last to sleep; she was more used to late nights than the rest, with the noise underneath her bedroom at home. She thought of her uncle at the counter and her father in the back, frying, sieving, banging the pans. And then the next she knew, it was day.

They went to the Big Pit, a disused Welsh coal-mine converted into a museum: which was not a line of smart underground show cases, but a real mine where the walls were dirty, the ceilings were low and the floor was uneven and trickled with water. Everyone wore a helmet with a modern Davy lamp, and it was very quiet under the hard hats as they went down in the big caged lift. Down, down, down, lower than going under the Thames tunnel, further down than anyone went up in the tower block lifts. And it was still very quiet as they walked along the 'roads' following their guide, who stooped as he would have had to stoop all the way to the pit face, going to dig coal. And when they were in a remote tunnel between two sets of closed fire doors he stopped, and said in his choky old Welsh voice, "Now turn off your lamps, will you? See for yourselves a drop of total darkness . . ."

The lights went off, each little searchlight on each hard head.

"You never see total darkness, you know. Not on the surface. There's always something, mind. But here you can't see a hand in front of your face. Can you?"

They tried – and they couldn't. The darkness was the blackest of blacks. It was awesome, had everybody silent for a bit, taking it in – with not even the breathing sounds of the night before, but tense shallow breaths. It was a new experience, something to make everyone think: and an instant of time when Kim Lung's mind went suddenly to when she'd heard talk about total darkness before, when she'd heard her father tell of it. Not underground like now, not in the west, but in a Vietnam night of a blackness never known in Britain. She remembered the talk about her mother and her father hiding in the jungle, waiting

with their group of refugees for the men who
would lead them to the mother boat. Twelve of
them from the south who had paid their gold to
the old man in the city, the twelve who had met
up by the sea and gone out in fishing boats to the
island off-shore. She remembered her dad telling

his brother of the moonless, starless darkness which had been so black, like now, that they had had to put their hands on the shoulders in front, so as not to get lost as they were led through the wet and slippery jungle. And how, to be counted by the boat man, they had had to stamp on the ground as they passed a certain spot because he couldn't see them.

And Kim had been there: not to be counted, but big in the total darkness of her mother's womb: knowing it only from what she had heard her father say afterwards.

As if suddenly attacked by a sharp pain, Kim shuddered, and in the dripping blackness of the mine she couldn't help but make the smallest of cries.

The lights came on.

"You all right, my pet? Wouldn't scare you for the world."

"Scaredy-pants!"

But Kim didn't seem to hear what Wendy said. She was shaking off the old, dark thought. That wasn't what she'd come on the School Journey for, to feel bad.

By the time they got back to the grey stone house which was the School Journey Centre, it was time for the evening meal: all scraping chairs and passing the water and the clatter of cutlery on plates. It had been a long day and nobody was too faddy to leave any of the hot-pot, mash and baked beans. Whole loaves disappeared like slices and no-one cleared their mouths to even mention missing their television. In what had been the dining room of the country mansion, used to best silver and cut-glass, Dockside School ate fast: taking the next mouthful before finishing the last, eyes much sharper for seconds of food than for the letters being dished out.

The post had come: a thin pack in a thick rubber band which had been delivered while they were down the Big Pit. Not a lot of it, it was only their second day away, but some children's parents had thought ahead and got letters and cards off

before the coach had left London.

"Just a few," said Mr Brewer, giving them out. "There'll be another post tomorrow . . ."

Kim watched Wendy open hers: saw her not bothering with the letter so much as the fiver folded up in it. How could she? She watched Joss with his card written in black italic script, laughing at some joke. And she watched Lyndsey sniffing at her pink Snoopy paper with its upside-down triangle of kisses. Then it was Duty Group, and washing up, and Kim was where she always spent a lot of her time – up to the wrists of her rubber gloves in a big kitchen sink, watching the suds.

4

The suds she watched the next day, though, were of a very different sort. Cold, frothing waves of them where they crashed in at the foot of the lifeboat cove. A glinty grey, the sea swelled itself up almost unseen, the wave shape becoming clear only at the last, just before it went thundering over the worn rocks.

The sea. Kim stared at it. She had never seen much of the sea. Her life had hardly taken her near it since she'd been born. She was much more used to the slow old Thames not far from the take-away – and that was very different to this. She stood apart and watched the water. She was held by it, because she knew it, the sea – in her bones, in her blood, in her soul. She was of the sea, was a true boat person: because Kim had been born on the mother boat.

She walked with the others round the lifeboat which had been designed to be so hard to sink. In its tight-fitting shed hung with medals and memorials to brave people, she looked at the powerful and sturdy craft, and she thought about that other one: the frail, overcrowded refugee boat. She thought about it in spite of herself, because she certainly didn't want to: no more than she'd wanted to think about that darkness in the Big Pit, which had started all of this off . . .

She remembered hearing her father telling his brother, when he had himself come to Britain. How he and her mother had been allowed on the mother boat with only the clothes they were wearing, everything else left behind on the island, every unnecessary weight, even the sandals from their feet. They had only been allowed the bottles of cough medicine everyone carried in their teeth, stuff to make them drowsy, to help them pass their difficult journey in sleep.

From high on the Welsh cliffs, Kim watched a small fishing boat bobbing out of the shelter of the cove. She heard the screams of the sea birds, each,

it seemed, with its own individual voice. And inside her head she imagined again the shouts and the screams of the people in the mother boat being told to be quiet by the sailors. Adults packed into the bottom where it was roughest and sickest, the elderly in the middle and the youngest on the top. Parents and their children separated: and with so many clamouring to go, no mother being certain that her child had been allowed to follow on. Names being called, backwards and forwards: shrieks of grief when no answers came, and louder shouts of anger from the sailors. Her father had told his brother about it in a flat voice as though it were a fact of life. And he had thought himself lucky, he'd said, because Hoa had her baby inside her, and people pushed to give her a little more room.

"Ain't you ever seen the sea before?" Lee was next to her: but not acting as rough as his voice. He was staring at the waves, too; and he put a hand on her shoulder.

"Not much," Kim said. And she was pleased he hadn't said it gentle, or she might have wanted to cry: not the point of a School Journey at all.

5

They were late back from the coast that evening and the warden wasn't pleased about it at all. Mrs Winterburn never grovelled to anyone, but she did go red when she saw the woman waiting for them at the front door. She shouted at the children to hurry – and she ended up serving the potatoes herself. So there was no time for the games on the field and in the woods that they'd been promised. It was wash up, diaries and bed.

And letters. They had time to get the post given out. Mr Brewer brought it round proudly as if he'd written it all himself – a fatter batch tonight with two rubber bands, one going each way.

The people who had had one the night before all had another, and most of the rest had one, too. There were posh-looking letters and tatty-looking letters; there were long ones and short ones; there were some with drawings put in by little brothers and sisters, some with money. Some were in

capital letters all through and didn't keep to the lines, some were faint and scrawly, and one was done on a computer. They came on white paper, on blue paper, on pink and rainbow: they were torn out, ripped off and crinkly-edged.

And nearly everyone got one. But Lee didn't, nor did Parveen: and neither did Kim.

"Early days," said Mr Brewer. "Tomorrow, eh?"

Kim went to bed, tucked in early, and turned her back on all the rude talk going on. The others thought she was too stuck up, but it wasn't that. She just couldn't forget that sea. She couldn't get out of her mind how that fishing boat in the Welsh cove had gone up and down on the water like a matchstick in her washing-up. She couldn't get out of her head the imaginary picture she had of her mother; imaginary because they hadn't even brought their sandals, let alone a photograph. And she began to get cross at her dad. Here she was, filled with sad thoughts which made her miss him – and he hadn't sent her a letter. All the children except three had heard from their homes, and she had to be one of the three! All of their parents were busy people, it wasn't just him. You could see how a lot of them had had a struggle with their ball-points and the paper. So why couldn't he have tried? It didn't need much. What sort of a father was he?

6

It was good in the back seat of the coach, going to
the farm. Especially for Kim because she wasn't
really a back-seat person: she was much more of
an up-front passenger. She didn't fight for a very
front seat or to sit next to a teacher, but she did
like to be where she could hear what they said,
and look at the things they pointed out. She'd sit
next to anyone – she often had to, because she
wasn't one of those glued to the same partner –
but she was surprised when it was Lee who
shouted, "Come on, Kim – up the back with me!"

And she'd gone. That had surprised her a bit,
too. Wendy went, and Tracy Sargent, and Jimmy
and a couple of others. But it was Lee who made
the fun, the one they really wanted to be with, and
it was Kim who he'd pushed in beside him,
squashed her beside the window.

Wendy didn't like it, that was as clear as a sheet
of cling-film. She mucked about all right, so did

Tracy, and they had a lot of laughs with Lee. But she didn't like it because most of what Lee said went Kim's way. And although they both gave him plenty of room for sliding closer, it was Kim he kept tight-to in the corner.

It was the letters, Kim decided: that was why he was being friendly. She hadn't had one, and he hadn't had one. With Parveen, who was up at the front with Narinder, they were a little band of three: and you did make friends with people who were the same as you. Last year the leavers had done it when they'd been told which secondary schools they were going to. School dinner and sandwich people did it all the time. And right now it was the letters: the not having them. It was a sort of comfort, like her family had, living close to other Vietnamese in London. But whatever the reason, Wendy Kent and Tracy Sargent didn't like it: they didn't like it one bit, staring at each other every time Kim spoke as if they didn't understand a word she said.

They liked the farm more. They forgot the coach for a bit when they went all soft over some of the animals, and it was very hard not to, with the newborn lambs like babies' toys, and the day-old calves like Bambis. They all went potty over one lamb which was being reared by another lamb's mother.

"That one's mother died," the girl from the farm told them. "But she's been accepted by that ewe."

"Aah! I'll have her," said Mr Brewer.

"Trust *ewe*! Get it? Ewe!"

They laughed. Mrs Winterburn was human after all: she'd cracked one! Everyone laughed except Kim – because in spite of herself she was having another of those sudden quiet moments; it was as if she was walking into them. She really didn't dwell on things as a rule – she got on. She worked hard at school and she worked hard at home downstairs in the take-away. Bed-time for her was never for staring at the ceiling and thinking about things, it was head on the pillow, turn over and sleep – usually in seconds. This week was turning out different, though: this week, standing and staring were part of the programme. And for her it was standing and staring and remembering . . .

Her mother had died, on the mother boat. Like the little lamb, Kim had been left to someone else to get her over those first dangerous days. She'd heard all about that through a thin wall, too. How, pregnant, hungry and worn out by the struggle and the strain of the escape, her mother had started having her on the boat, weeks early. How the boat had hit heavy seas and people had been thrown about and crushed in the tossing and rolling. How Kim had been born and her mother had died. And how another woman with a young child had shared her breast milk.

"Baa! You look like one of them. Don't she look like one of them, staring?" Wendy Kent was a bad enemy to make. Things went her way, or they went off. "Sheep-face!"

Big Eddie, the one Wendy was talking to, smirked his smirk. "Baa!" he agreed.

"Cleverest thing you've said all week," Kim told him. And her back stayed straight: because she was her mother's daughter, and this sort of thing was nothing to what that brave woman had gone through.

7

There was time for games that night, up on the sloping meadow they called the sports field. Organised games: football and rounders, until three rounders balls had been lost in the undergrowth on the edge and they started asking for something else. Hide and seek in the thick woods above them.

"Tomorrow, the last night," promised Mr Brewer. "Can't be late for supper twice."

They were kept waiting to go in for their meal: a bit of pay-back from the warden, probably. But while they queued, to stop them getting noisier and noisier, Mr Brewer came down the line with the letters which had come that day. And it was a very thick handful. Eyes really stared, everyone's eyes, even those of people pretending to look the other way. And there seemed to be something for everyone. For some it was the third and fourth they'd had, for Parveen it was the first – and it was the first for a red-faced Lee, whose tooth-gap smile would have made a photograph worth framing.

Something for everyone, it seemed, except Kim. At the meal table with only her plate to concentrate on, she found it hard to get her food down. All the talk around her was of London and what was going on at home; pets and grans and the telly; everyone showing this bit and that in their letters: all whispered secrets and loud jokes and ketchup on the envelopes. Debbie had got a letter from a boy she said she didn't like in the third year, written somewhere private on lavatory

paper. Pulling it out too quickly, she had to share
it with her table, every soppy page ending 'NOW
PLEASE WASH YOUR HANDS'. Mrs
Winterburn read out her husband's views on the
new council swimming pool: and Mr Brewer
tucked a letter down his jumper. But there was
nothing for Kim, not until the teachers noticed
and they found a postcard from Mr Holt for her to
be in charge of.

It gave her indigestion, her disappointment. Her
rotten dad! How old was she? How long had he
been in England? Couldn't he have put himself
out to learn enough English in ten years to write
'Dear Kim. Love from Dad' – how hard was that
to do? It was all she wanted. He could have sent

his signature written sideways down one of their menus and made her feel good. But nothing: he'd sent nothing. He was a great failure. Why couldn't he try harder and find the guts to go to classes, even if they were difficult? Why did he always have to lean on her? What sort of a rotten father was he?

"Oi! Kim – what's this say?"

It was Lee. They'd been dismissed and he had found her in the little ornamental garden with the view of the sparkling valley: the quiet place with no ball games where no-one went. He had got his mother's letter, was still grinning with it – but he couldn't read it very well.

Kim helped him. And, somehow, it helped her. In spite of her dark mood, she found herself settling into it. It was interesting how people were different. She had a dad and no mum; Lee had a mum and no dad, just uncles who came on different days. They all sent their best to him, signed their different names and put a few jokes in. Otherwise, the letter was all about the music charts and what was happening in the serials. A different life to hers. And the letter ended with more kisses than Kim could count.

There was a secret sound from the rockery above them.

"Here they are! Look at them two! Know you now!"

Kim needn't have looked to know whose jealous voice that was: Wendy – pointing, sneering, twisting up her face for Tracy. Why? She was only helping Lee, it wasn't any more than that. But before she could explain it, try to make friends again, Wendy went. She pulled Tracy away as if she had something urgent to do. Probably something nasty to Kim's bed.

"Cheers, mate." And Lee had gone, too.

The sun was casting shadows on the valley now, the sparkle had all gone from this place. Kim went to the kitchen to help Mr Brewer with the cocoa. And then she went to check her bed. But all Wendy ended up doing was to ignore it, with Kim in it. She talked loudly all round her, and was careful not to answer the couple of quiet words Kim said.

8

The next day they went to the castle at Goodrich.
But their clipboards had been carried round a lot
of places by then – and what really had them
buzzing was the 'wide game' when they got back.
Not just ordinary hide and seek, Mr Brewer
promised, but something bigger, with teams and
proper rules. It was to be their last night there. No
diaries and follow-up work as everyone who
wanted to went up to the field to join in.

Mr Brewer explained it all carefully. Half the
group were to go off into the woods to hide.
They'd be quite safe, he told them: the woods
were bounded by a strong fence on their further
side so there was no danger of anyone wandering
off the site. The other half of the group would
count a hundred and then go out looking for them,
with a few good tacklers staying behind to guard
the home base – which was Mrs Winterburn and
the anoraks. Every hider who got back scored a

point. Everyone who was 'had' gave a point to the hunting side. And anyone who stayed hidden till the end scored half a point when the three whistles sounded.

Those were the rules, and Kim was herded by Mr Brewer's arm into one of the groups of prey. She didn't play out of doors much where she lived, her father wouldn't let her, so this was something different. When the whistle went for the start, she ran off fast with the others, high-stepped in her wellingtons through the stingers and the fern, and quickly decided on a course of her own to the left. Everyone who went together would get found together, she reckoned. She could get a point on her own. With a quick look back over her shoulder to check who was watching who, who was going where, she disappeared into the darkness of her side of the woods. But already her heart had sunk — because what she had seen when she looked around was Wendy and Tracy and Big Eddie coming out to the edge of the group that was left, on her side of the field. So! Her new enemies were going to be her hunters.

They weren't pointing, they weren't showing by

anything very much which way they were looking, but Kim knew very well who those three were going to come after: it was definitely going to be her. She was their target, she was going to be their prey. And who would care about the rules? The real idea, what they'd really be after, was to find her, and get her and hurt her – accidentally push her over in the nettles, something like that. She knew from the way they'd been standing – all casual and pretending not to look, but smiling – that hurting her was what their game was all about.

She ran hard through the moist and slippery wood, quickly decided to go off the wide path onto the narrow track. Then off the narrow track into the undergrowth till she was crashing through tangles of bush and spiders' webs that had had nothing come their way for a year. The voices of the other hiders went distant as she looked desperately for a place well away from where Wendy might look. All she could hear as she jumped and pushed was the thump of her heart and the sounds of the fears in her head. She didn't want a quick run-in. The last thing she was after now was a point. All she wanted was to stay hidden and to get safely back to supper without any kicking or punching or scratching or stinging: without any of the things those others were out to do to her.

Cleverly, it struck her as she ran that her best protection might be the very thing she was frightened of: nettles and thorns. If she didn't like them, the hunters wouldn't either, would they? Getting tired now, legs heavy in her boots, she saw what she thought might do. Coming at it by a roundabout way so as not to show where she'd gone in, Kim crept and crawled and weaved herself into the biggest blackberry bush she could find. A blackberry bush very dense and prickly, a careful hiding place where she daren't move once she was lying there because to move would be to scratch herself badly. She lay there, thought of a million better places the way hiders do, but knew she had to stick with that one. And like that, trembling, Kim waited.

And lying there, not thinking about anything but her fear, she knew for sure what it had been like on that island in Vietnam. Not from the stories she'd heard when her father told his brother, but from being pressed against the earth right here. She could have been her father, and these hunters could have been the North Vietnamese soldiers brought south to stop him getting away from that island, searching the jungle with orders to capture or to kill.

She could have been her father lying there, his wife beside him, both scared to death in the pitch darkness. The soldiers wouldn't be blamed for killing, these guards crashing through the foliage with their weapons out to use.

34

"We're right here! We know you're there! Give up! Come on, give up!"

"Can you hear us? It's you we're coming for!"

Was it bluff? Mental warfare? Which way were the footsteps coming?

9

As she'd hoped they wouldn't, but dreaded they would, they came her way. Wendy Kent and Tracy Sargent came with a grudge against her over Lee, bringing Big Eddie with them to do what they wanted. And from their voices when she heard them in the distance, she knew she'd been right over what they were about.

"Snobby little dilk!"

"Show-off! Anyhow, all sorts happen when you fall over!"

"Yeah, bad luck, eh?!"

They laughed, looking forward to hurting her.

"Only be her word against ours!"

And then it was Wendy in a witch voice with the worst of hide-and-seek scares, calling out. "We know you're here! You can hear us, can't you? We're coming to get you!"

Kim didn't move. She couldn't be sure how well she'd tucked her left foot under the bush behind her, but she knew she couldn't shift it. She couldn't make a movement, not run the risk of a sound. They were getting closer now, only metres away; they'd done horribly well to follow her trail. She could hear their breathing, could almost feel their strong will to find her and hurt her. In despair she clawed her fingers into the cold soil, allowed an insect into her ear, stopped breathing normally and took shallow breaths which wouldn't move her back. It wasn't what she wanted to do.

She wanted to jump up and scream. Instead, it was a fight to stay still. But she fought hard, made her eyes know the sight, her nostrils the smell, her mouth the taste of the earth she was pressed so hard against.

"You hear us, Kim Lung? We're gonna get you!"

Closer. Very close. A sudden risked move, the lift of an eye. And the sight of the toe-cap of a boot so close the stitching could be counted. A cringe, a wait for the shout, for the blow – but holding the breath, fighting not to panic.

But it would only be a fist, or a boot. It wouldn't be a bayonet. It wouldn't be what her father had had: a bayonet stabbing down into the dense foliage and into his hand, into the flesh between his finger and his thumb; pinning him to the rotting earth while still he didn't shout; holding it, twisting it, then pulling it away to be stabbed into the next big plant – only the darkness hiding the blood on the soldier's bayonet.

Kim's heart beat enough to lift her body from the ground. She closed her eyes again, did her screaming inside her head, like her father had done.

And then suddenly it wasn't a scream but a whistle which sounded, three blessed times. And crashing away on a run-in from some distant place of his own came Lee, whooping in a winning way.

"Didn't get me! Half a point, I got!"

"Stupid game!" said Big Eddie. "Get a football

out, eh?"

"Yeah – when I got me half a point!"

The two boys went off: so did Wendy and Tracy, after one last hard look round.

"Thought she'd come this way."

"Done a double back."

"Yeah. Leave it."

They ran off. But it was a very long time before Kim could emerge. It seemed to take her a lifetime to come crawling out of that hiding place.

10

When the coach drew up at the school everyone
on the pavement waved as if it were a royal visit.
Dogs had come, and push-chairs with little
brothers and sisters. Mr Holt, the headteacher,
was there, smiling a welcome. But it was the
parents' faces everyone wanted to see. No eyes
were ever sharper than in that first look along
Dockside for the people they lived with.

Kim, too: eyes sharper today than anyone's. And
he was there, her father, smiling shyly, waving his
hand in a small and private way. Kim saw him
and didn't push to be first off the coach. She
didn't need to. He was there, everything was all
right, she could wait. She looked out of the
window as she queued in the aisle, and she waved
again. Back came another smile, an ordinary smile,
a smile with nothing of an apology for not writing,
just pleased to see her.

She blew him a little kiss. Well, it was her fault,

too, wasn't it? She'd worked it out last night. She hadn't bothered to translate that bit about the letters, said at the end of the meeting. She'd had enough by then – so how was he to know? And she hadn't thought she'd *need* a letter from him. She could easily have left him with a couple of envelopes already addressed: but she hadn't thought she'd miss him.

At last her turn came. She jumped off the coach and surprised him with her hug, almost pulled him over. He hugged her in return and took a step back, shook his head at her. Well, why should he understand this loving? He wasn't to know this was her secret way of saying sorry for those bad thoughts she'd had about him. He wasn't to know what she knew now – that he wasn't a man of words and writing, but a man of action. A brave man those years ago, and a strong man now, a good example of how they all had to be in London. No-one remembered what had happened in Vietnam any more: no-one seemed to know, even, or to care.

But Kim did. She understood it now. And as they walked to the bus, she made sure he had her case in his good hand, and she changed places on the pavement, to get a tight hold on his bayonet scar.